Words Are Healing

Angellica S

Presentation by *BookLeaf Publishing*

Web: www.bookleafpub.com

E-mail: info@bookleafpub.com

Find Angellica S on:
Instagram @angellicawrites
Twitter @angellicawrites
Tiktok @angellicawrites
Goodreads: Angellica S
Contact: author@angellica.com.au

ISBN: 9789357447522

First edition 2022

DEDICATION

To those who need borrowed words.

ACKNOWLEDGEMENT

I'd like to thank the universe for granting me a way to share my words left unsaid.

PREFACE

Poetry is an art unlike any other.
Poetry is an expression of the heart and soul,
crafted by the mind.
Poetry has allowed me to speak when I wished
not to.

I present to you a collection of poems that may
find resonance inside others—or not.

Either way, words are healing.

Remembering Is Hard When All You Can Do Is Forget

You! Time-traveller.
You treat me so differently—cosplaying
childhood.
As if you're attempting to fix all of those years
that long ago passed, spilled onto empty, unseen
pages.
Pages of the mind; a book organ.
You pump my lifeline through your paper.
I
don't
remember
telling you to
forget me—to forget
my most precious memories.

Oh, time traveller, how did you get here?

Germination of the Soul

Branches
to show you what you became.
Roots
to show you where you remain.
Nails
to remind you of the pain
you suffered—at your own hands.
Feet
to show you where you stand.
Teeth
to remind you that you can bite.
Fists
a reminder that you can fight
against all the pain
you gain
time and time
again.

The Power of Hours

Time.

I watch as it streams out of the faucet
—the sink in the bathing chamber.

Time, streaming out of the faucet,
as I stand there—unmoving.

I am time.

I can't seem to grasp
how these words will get out of me
in time to reach your ears.
Your eyes.

I am the oldest I have ever been;
I will never be this young again.

My fingers have a mind of their own.

I do not control these words, They do—
time.

A Prescription for Sanity

Spilling my last breaths
onto your surface.
Bright white—
You saved me.

My Rorschach,
unveil me viewer.
Look into the darkest parts of
my Soul.

I accept my true form.
Do you, viewer?
No?
Do you, reader?

Could I ask you a question?
I must ask for your confidentiality, Doctor.
Could you do that for me?
…Thank you.

Do you…know what's wrong?
With me, that is.

Detective, can you help her?
I need you to solve a cold case.

Should I feel guilty?
Guilty for enjoying the silence
that caresses my ears when the world is sleeping.
The world…all but me that is.

Or at least it feels that way.
You'll find a machine in me, doctor.
Not one that can be removed, however.
A machine

Fuelled by silence.
A machine
fuelled by soundless nights,
harmless frights…

Dr, am I guilty?

Sincerely,
a concerned patient, awaiting answers.

The Way You're Always in Your Head

The way that the world turns,
is the way that
my stomach turns

when I see you,

smiling to yourself
when you think
that nobody else

can see you.

A Crime of Passion

What would happen
if today
was the day
that I—

what if today
was the day
that I…
decided to leave,

taking your last breath with you.
Your chance of survival—
gone.
I took it with me.

What if I left you defenceless
against a one-person-storm.
A storm that arrived
whenever one half of a whole

walked out the door.
A quarrel of love
is a quarrel of fate.
A quarrel of love

is a happening that could
start-all or end-all.
What if I left you—
barely breathing,

as I—as I—
as I started a new life for myself.
One half of a whole,
becoming whole.

What would happen if I
left you your half of a whole?
Would you become whole again,
like me?

Or would you crumble…
a half becoming nothing.
Dust in a storm;
A storm of love.

Healed now, I look behind me.
I was once told,
to never leave my back towards
my enemies...

but there is something about it that feels so—
innately right.
I can't see you but…
it's right…right?

I don't remember telling you to forget me.

To forget us.

But, this is right…right?

The Denouement

If I were to put my finger in front of the clock's
hand,
my final act would be cleaning.

God, how I hate cleaning.
There is something so mundane—
so insane—about tidying.

I'd start with my sleeping chambers—
top to bottom with the duster!

Watching the clock tick for the last time,
my fated finger's actions—already foretold
by myself.

I hope, in this moment, that maybe—
just maybe—
you'd see this hospital chamber—
not a spot in sight…

and remember me as someone that I'm not.

Wishes of the Wicked

I used to long for broken bones,
and broken homes
and kidney stones.

I used to long for sleepless nights,
and useless frights
and lungs—air-tight.

I used to dream of a life for me
where you could see
who I could be.

I used to long for a life like this—
but not for mine,
for that was too fine.

But now, arms outstretched,
reaching for my words—
snatching from the birds

who fly above;

a pigeon, a dove,
a 'pie who flew straight up into the sky.

I take it back,
please hear my pleads.
I take it back.
I take it back.

Weeps of the Wicked

I can smell it.
My window—
half cracked;

I can smell the weeps of the wicked.
The weeps of the wicked…
Oh, how they haunt me!

On my nose,
your tears find safety.
I'll be Your bucket,

just for today.

A Run-in with the Man-in-blue

I don't have anything—
not for You, Officer.

Do you know why?

You police my thoughts;
my words are not of interest to you.

I am not of interest to you…

A plain face,
in the face of death

I am a blank canvas,
awaiting my brushstrokes.

No soul lives inside that canvas,
Officer.

Nobody is home.
At least, no one of interest to You.

Don't come crawling to me—
in a year—full of fear.

Don't come crying when your case is cold
because the case was always cold.

That canvas never had brushstrokes,
even though there appears to be a smudge on the
front.

In fact, that case never existed, Officer.

Officer, what are you talking about?
You're scaring me…

There's nobody there, Officer.
Who is this girl you speak of?

He looks around.

"She—"
She was everywhere
and no where.

"I'm sorry, it appears I've made a mistake."

A Distortion of Fate

You hate me

    And I, you.

You see me in you.

    I see me in you too.

My eyes, they mirror yours.

    Your eyes, they dissect me.

When will it be My turn?
My time to live.
My time to run.

When will it be My tapestry
that is to be spun.

When will it be my turn…
to be real?

Who Am I to You…?

I am not him, nor have I ever been.
You seem to forget that—often.
I wonder, what is it about me that makes you see him.
Is it my voice? My hands? My face? This place?
Is it the way the door bangs when I come home?
The sound—echoing through the house?
No? I suppose not.
I suppose it's my foot—boot clad, that is.
Do you dream of my boot on your neck?
Do you dream of my shouts of anger?
I don't think I'll ever be able to place it.
Why do you see him when you look at me?
I am not your father, girl,
nor will I ever be.
I will not coddle you in my arms,
when it is you who brings upon all of my
qualms.
If anything, it should be I who sees the ill in you.
You come and you go, but I question
whether you were ever here…
Your eyes—oh so distant…so very unclear.

Darling, I am not your Daddy.
Nor will I ever be.

The Town's Water Fountain

I am the town's fountain. I am the town's well.
Every night it rains. And I gather it.
I fill myself up with water
because You need water to live.
And I need water to be able to give You water to
live.

All because I do not exist if I have nothing to
give.
I would give anything to make You happy.
I am the town's water fountain. I am your well.
I provide. You thrive. But I cannot survive
a life where all I do is give.

No matter how much it rains, I feel empty.
No amount of water will make me feel whole.
No amount of water will save my dead soul.
I am the town's fountain. I will always be so.
But just because a town has one fountain doesn't
mean

it shouldn't have another. Perhaps that's what I
need.
Another fountain to help catch water.
Maybe—maybe if there were two of us…
Yes. I think perhaps that might do the trick.
I think two fountains may be what You need.

Since I am not enough for You.
Why do You bleed me dry of water?
Every day to no end. It's the same.
Vampire—vampire, stalking a dame.
Vampire drinking the blood 'til her brain

can no longer produce such meaningful words
as those on a page. Ink spills at Your words.
I am the town's water fountain.
But that's not enough. That's not enough
because You are too rough

with me,
the town's water fountain.

Words of the Mind

There is a certain beauty
in the way the mind drifts.

From flowers to powers—
wandering words, for hours.

I often wonder,
what it would be like if it didn't…

A mind empty is no mind at all,
they so claim.

But, you have to admit…
it would be rather serene, wouldn't it?

To be able to lay on that comforter of clouds,
at peace with the world around you.

No worries from the day—
words you didn't mean to say.

But there's a certain beauty
in the way the mind drifts.

How a thought so often slips,

from your parted resting lips

of the mind.
The mouth inside—

it consumes.

My Shadow

The one I loved.
The one I craved.
The one who comes out once a day.
When the sun is up
and the lights are out.
Who comes out whenever I do doubt

whether it is real…
what we have—
what I feel.
Your dark silhouette—
before you,
I'd kneel.

You are my knight,
shining armour and all.
You'd always come
if I happened to call.
But that's not possible—
'caus you are not tangible;

A shadow on my wall.
You stand—Oh, so tall.
So comforting is your presence—
Your dark encompassing essence.

You hug me.
You hold me.

You are me,
my shadow.

The Cenote Inside My Soul

I love to be unloved
while I drown
in my underwater cave.

I become a fish—
metamorphosis.
In my self-built grave.

I become something I am
when no one is looking.

In the water's reflection…
that is where you'll find me.

Staring into the eyes
of the one who hurt me most.

Escaping Fate

June birds soared across oceans
the first time I heard you say my name.

Except, what ARE June birds?
A figment of my imagination, perhaps?
Or a chemical reaction?

Death visited me in a dream once…
he told me when I'd die—I didn't…

Except he didn't specify the time.
How odd, you'd think a man with that much
responsibility,
and that much experience…
you'd think he'd be more organised.

I'm sitting here now, on that day.
Maybe it will happen in my sleep.

Three weeks and one day.
That day was yesterday, now.

I like to think I could've, though.
Maybe in another reality, another version of me
passed.

I've been blindsided.

Clotho, May I See How My Story Ends?

My own personal mask and cape—
my face.
My fate—
I can't escape.
My faith
is slipping—
dripping
from the faucet.
Tears
streaming
down
the drain—
again,
again,
again
and again.